RECORDED VERSIONS
GUITAR ®

AUTHENTIC TRANSCRIPTIONS
WITH NOTES AND TABLATURE

Sarah McLachlan

Mirrorball

Artwork designed by John Rummen for Artwerks
Photography by Al Robb   Used by Permission

Music transcriptions by Pete Billmann, Steve Gorenberg, Jeff Perrin and Jeff Story

ISBN 0-634-01099-9

HAL•LEONARD®
CORPORATION
7777 W. BLUEMOUND RD. P.O. BOX 13819 MILWAUKEE, WI 53213

Visit Hal Leonard Online at
www.halleonard.com

Building a Mystery

Words and Music by Sarah McLachlan and Pierre Marchand

* Gtr. 1 chord symbols
** Gtr. 2 chord symbols
† Symbols in parentheses represent chord names respective to capoed guitars.
Symbols above reflect actual sounding chords. Capoed fret is "0" in TAB.
Chord symbols reflect basic tonality.

Verse

come out of night, that's when the en-er-gy comes __ and the dark side's __ light __ and the vam-pire's __ roam. __ You strut your ras-ta wear __ and your su-i-cide __ po-em and a

4

Verse

live in a church where you sleep with voo-doo dolls and you won't give up the search for the

ghosts in the halls. You wear san-dals in the snow and a smile that won't wash a way.

Can you look out the win-dow with-out your shad-ow get-ting in the way?

6

To Coda ⊕

build-ing ___ a mys-ter - y ___ and choos - ing ___ so ___ care -

- ful - ly.

3. You woke up

Verse

scream-ing a-loud, ___ a prayer_ from your _ se-cret god ___ you feed off our _ fears ___ and

echo off

pitch: D#

8

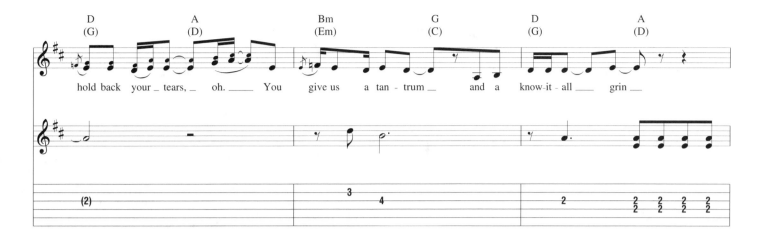

hold back your _ tears, _ oh. _____ You give us a tan - trum _ and a know-it - all ___ grin ___

D.S. al Coda

$\oplus$ *Coda*

just when you need one _ when the eve - ning's thin. _____

Gtr. 1: w/ Rhy. Fill 1

care - ful - ly. _____
care - ful - ly.)

Gtr. 3

* Male vocals written *8vb* throughout.

Guitar Solo

Gtr. 3 tacet
(C/G)   Dsus4/A)   (C/G)   (Csus2) (A5)
Gtr. 1

(Oo, _____ oo.

Gtr. 2

f

** w/ wah-wah

1/2

** Wah used as a filter, next 4 meas.

Rhy. Fill 1
Gtr. 1

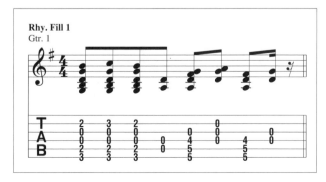

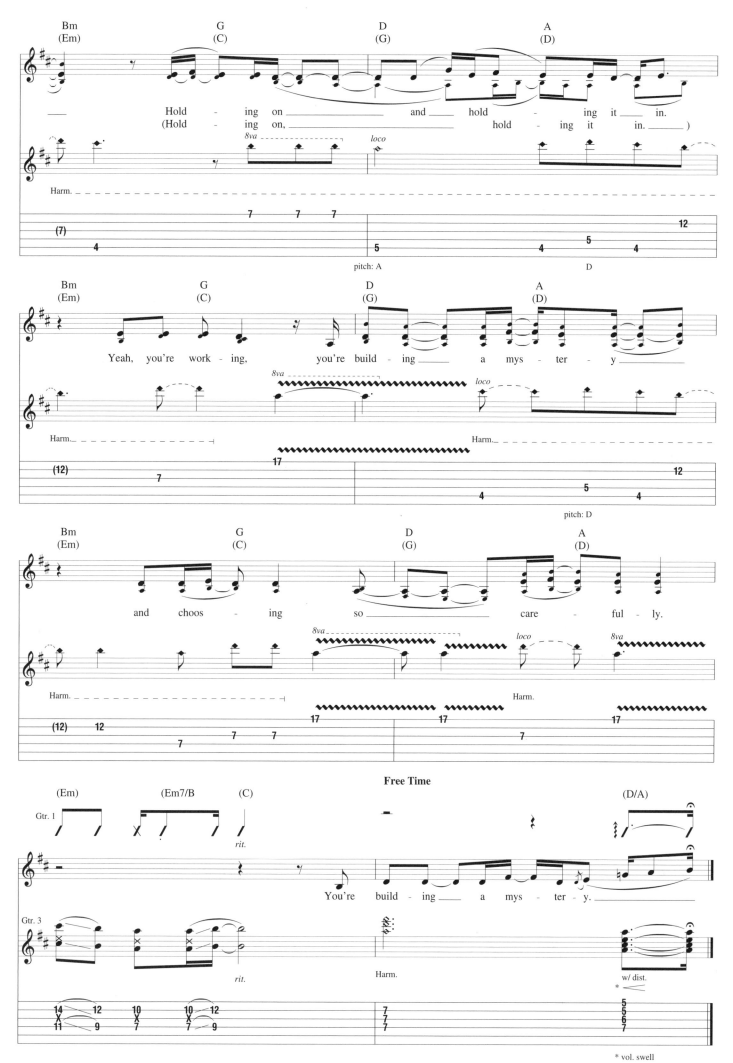

Hold On

Words and Music by Sarah McLachlan

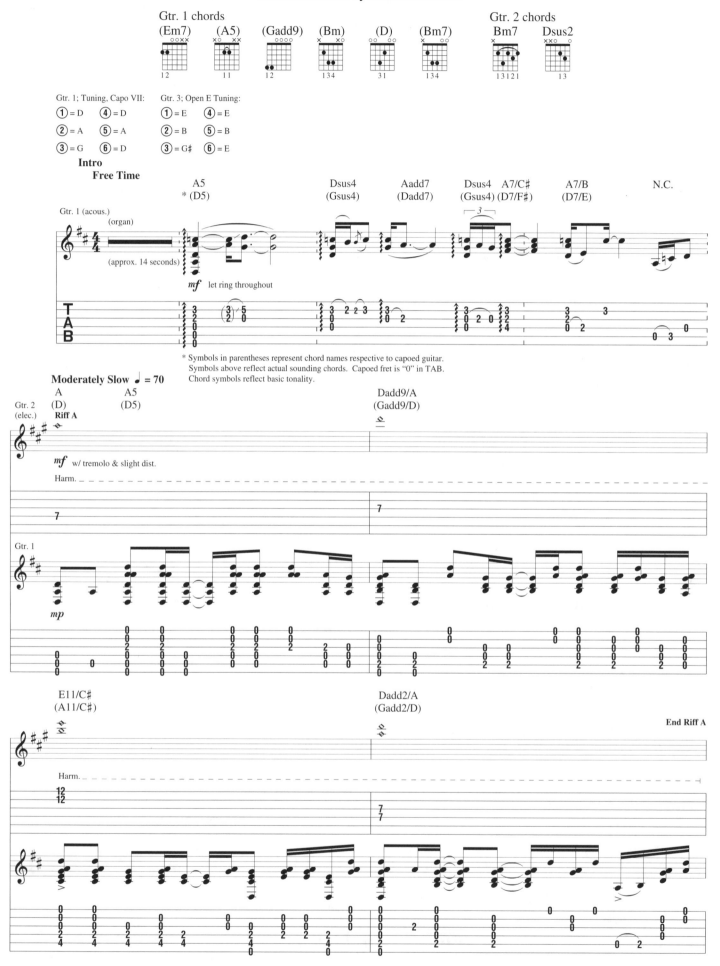

Verse

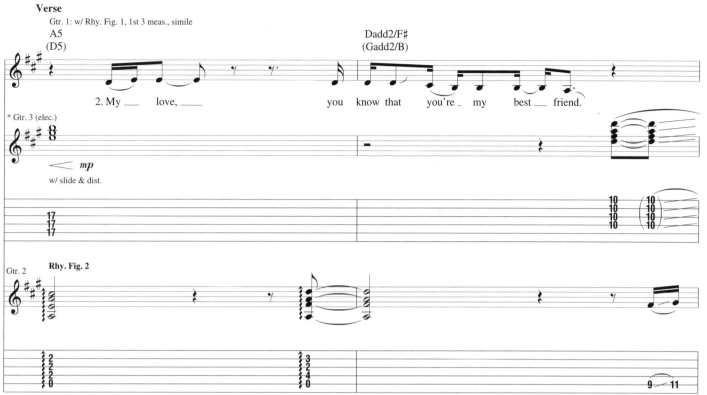

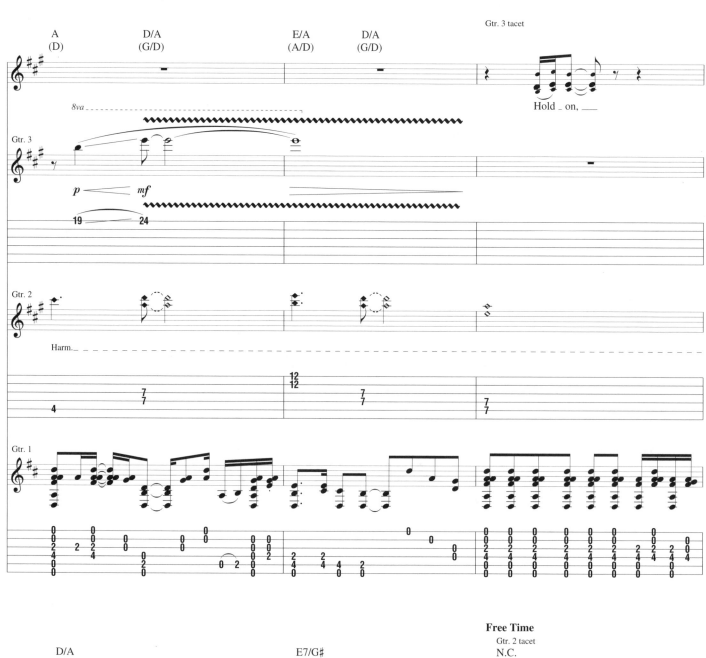

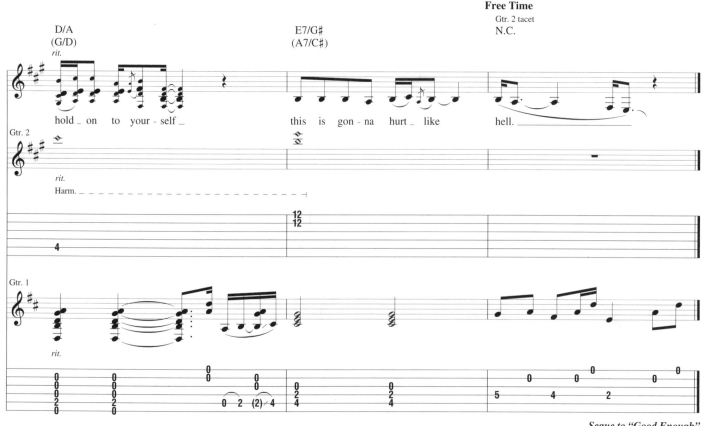

Segue to "Good Enough"

Good Enough

Words and Music by Sarah McLachlan

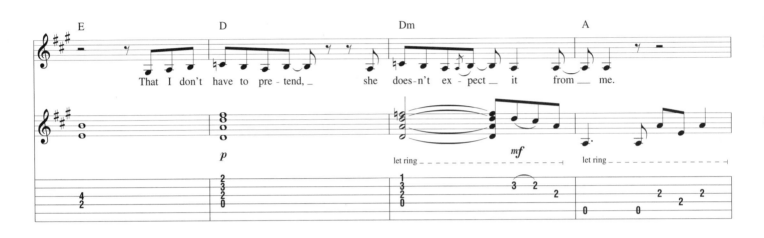

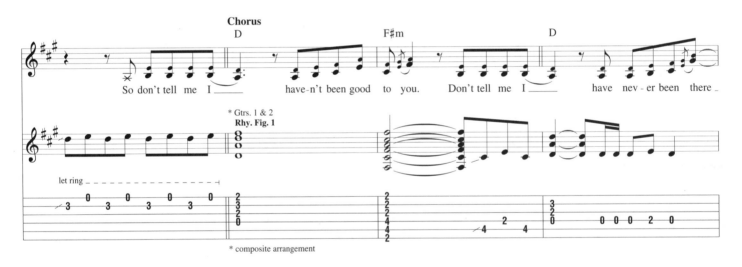

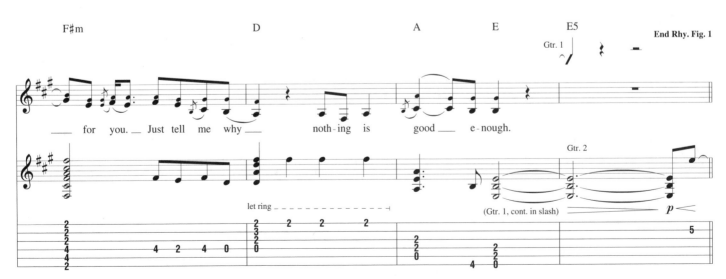

* Male vocals sung *8vb.*

Chorus

for ___ you. I'll show you why ___ you're so much more _____ than good ___ e-nough.   Ah.

Outro-Guitar Solo

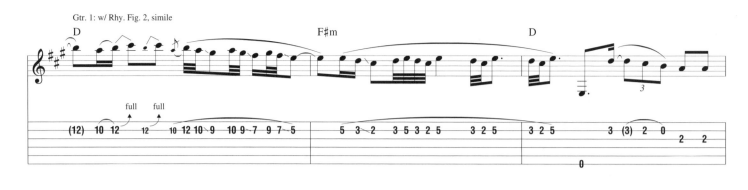

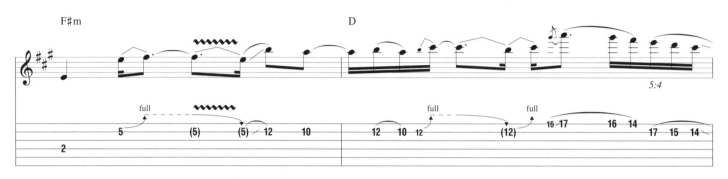

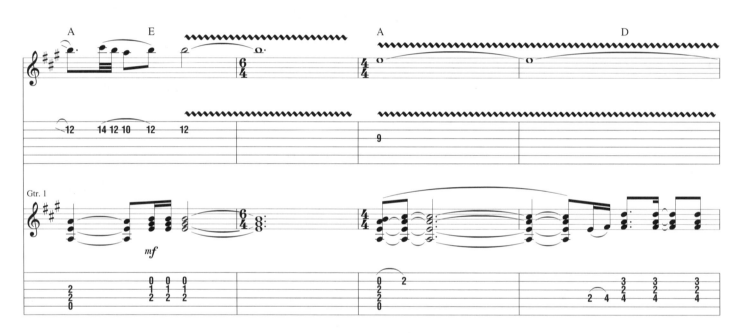

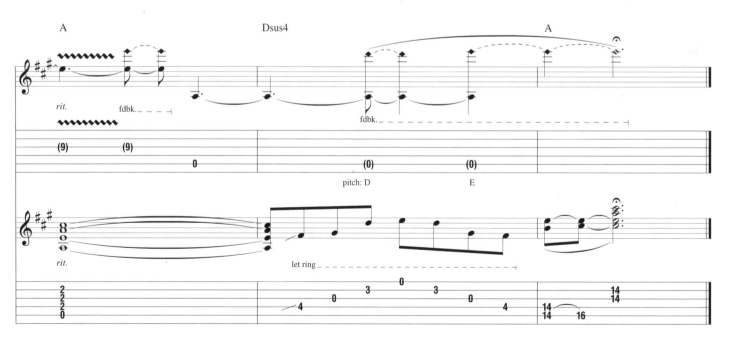

I Will Remember You

Theme from *THE BROTHERS McMULLEN*

Words and Music by Sarah McLachlan, Seamus Egan and Dave Merenda

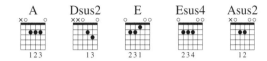

* Piano arr. for gtr.
** Chord symbols reflect basic tonality.

* T = Thumb on ⑥

A   A/D   E7   A

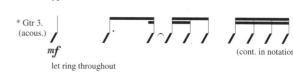

Weep not ___ for _____ the mem - o - ries. _____

* Two gtrs. arr. for one.

Verse

1. I'm ___ so _____ tired, ___ but I can't sleep. ___ Stand-in' on the edge _ of some - thin'

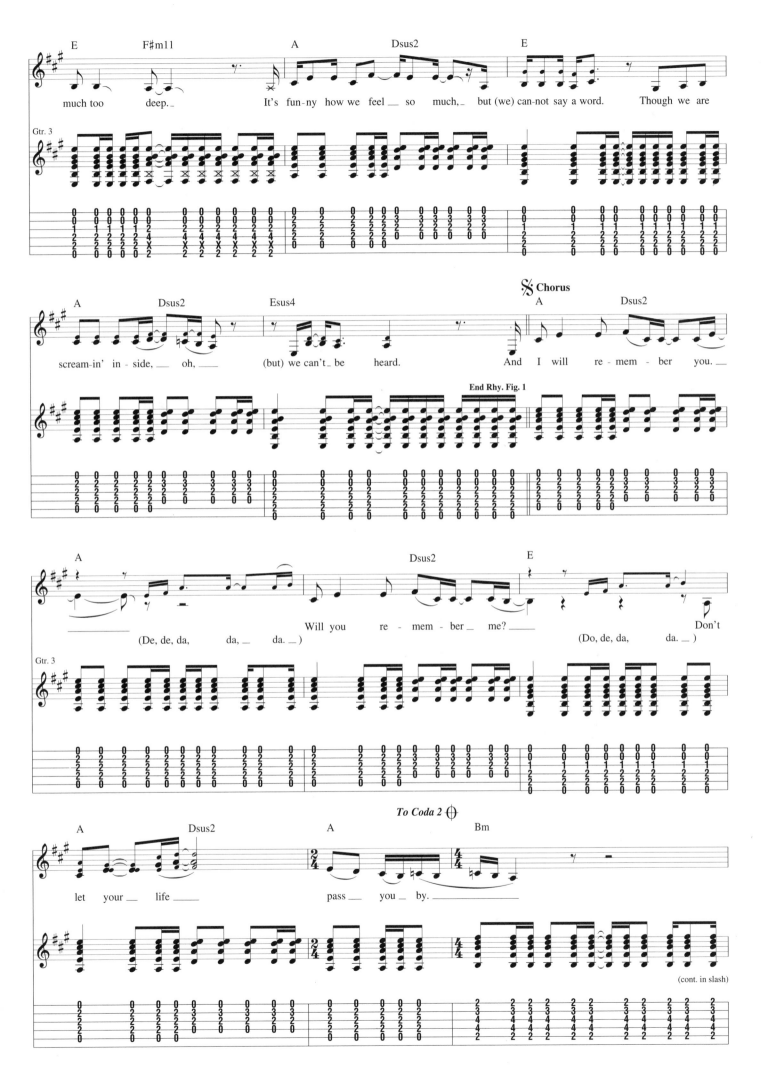

Adia

Words and Music by Sarah McLachlan and Pierre Marchand

Gtr. 2 chords

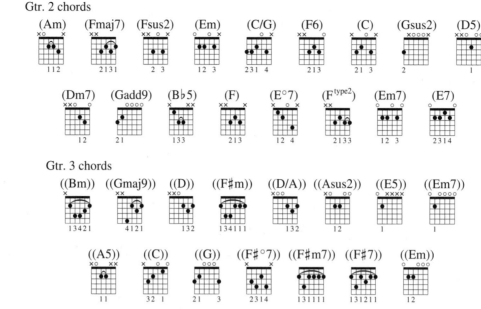

Gtr. 3 chords

Gtr. 2; Tuning, Capo III:
① = D   ④ = D
② = A   ⑤ = A
③ = G   ⑥ = E

Gtrs. 1 & 3: Capo I

Verse
Moderately Slow ♩ = 82

1. A - di - a, I do___ be - lieve___ I failed___ you.___

* Chord symbols reflect overall tonality.

A - di - a, I know___ I've let___ you down.___

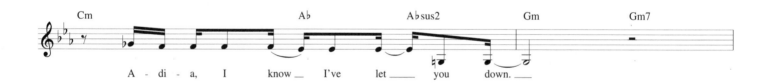

Don't you know I tried___ so hard___ to love you in___ my way?___   It's

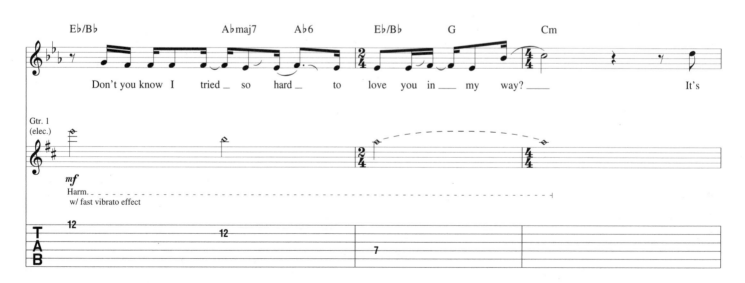

Gtr. 1 (elec.)

mf
Harm.
w/ fast vibrato effect

* Symbols in parentheses represent chord names respective to capoed guitar.
Symbols above reflect actual sounding chord. Capoed fret is "0" in TAB.

Verse

* Chords in double parentheses played by Gtr. 3 throughout.

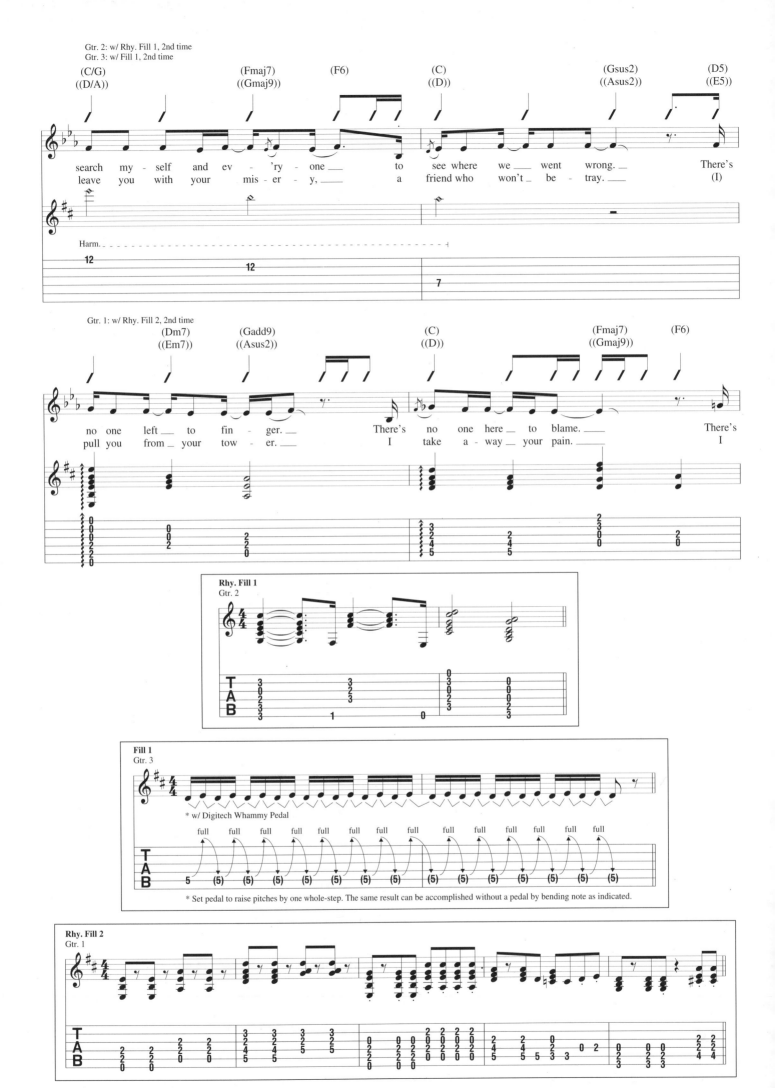

40

I Love You

Words and Music by Sarah McLachlan

* Played behind the beat.

*Symbols in parentheses represent chord names respective to capoed guitar. Symbols above reflect actual sounding chord. Capoed fret is "0" in TAB.

Do What You Have to Do

Words and Music by Sarah McLachlan and Colleen Wolstenholme

* Piano arr. for gtr.

** Chord symbols reflect basic tonality.

your soul. and burn - ing slow, ___ I'm ev - er swift - ly mov - ing, and deep with - in I'm shak - en by the vi -

Gtr. 1: w/ Rhy. Fill 1, 2nd time

try'n' to ___ es - cape this ___ de - sire. ___ The
- 'lence of ex - ist - ing for on - ly you. ___ I

A Tempo

Gtr. 1: w/ Rhy. Fig. 1, simile

yearn - ing to be near you, } I do what ___ I have to do. ___
know I can't be with you, }

Oh, the yearn-in' to be near you,
Oh, I know I can't be with you,

I do what I have ____ to ____

Chorus
Gtr. 1: w/ Rhy. Fig. 2, simile

____ do. But I had the sense ____ to

To Coda ⊕

rec - og - nize ____ that I don't ____ know ____ how to let ____ you ____ go. ____

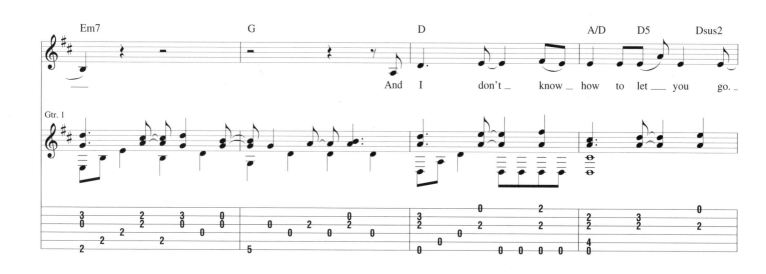

And I don't ___ know ___ how to let ___ you go. ___

Gtr. 1

Coda

Don't _ know _ how _ to let _ you _ go, _ don't _ know how _

Gtr. 1

cresc.

Free Time

to let you _ go. _ And I don't _ know

how to let you _____ go.

The Path of Thorns (Terms)

Words and Music by Sarah McLachlan

*Symbols in parentheses represent chord names respective to capoed guitar. Symbols above reflect actual sounding chord. Capoed fret is "0" in TAB.

*composite arrangement

MCA Music Publishing

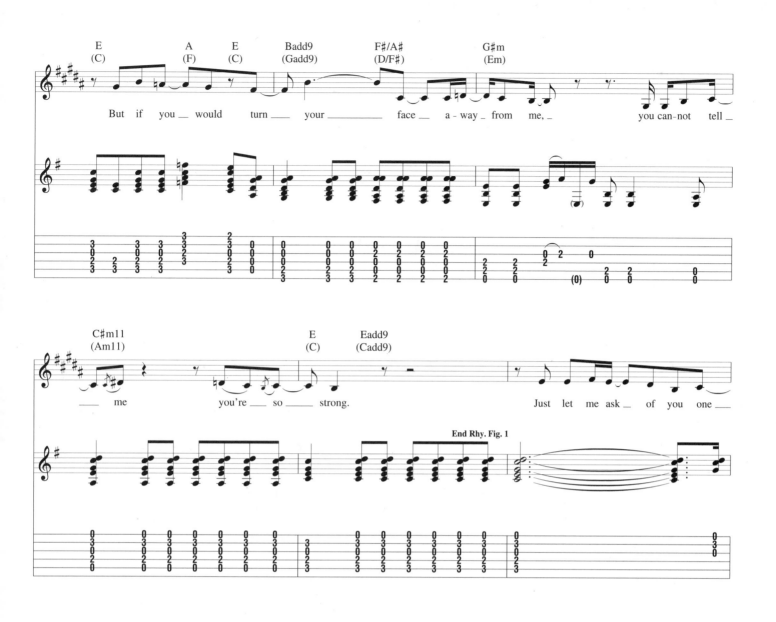

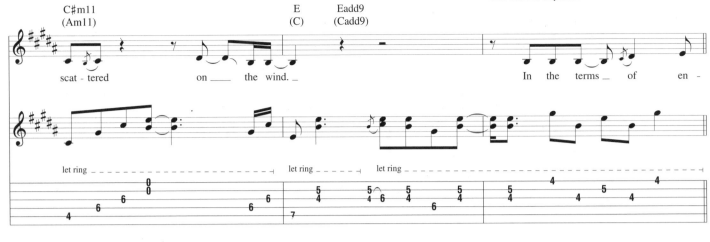

Chorus

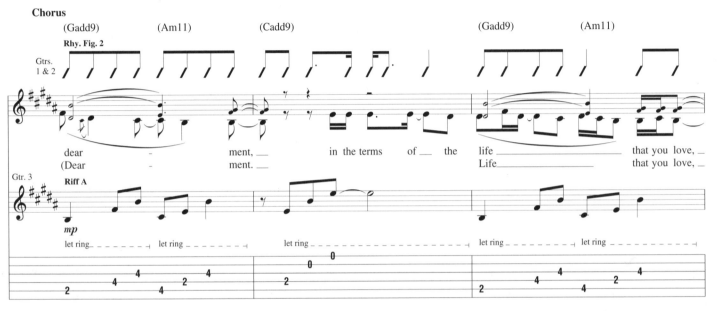

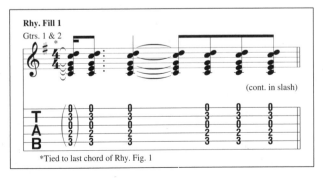

*Tied to last chord of Rhy. Fig. 1

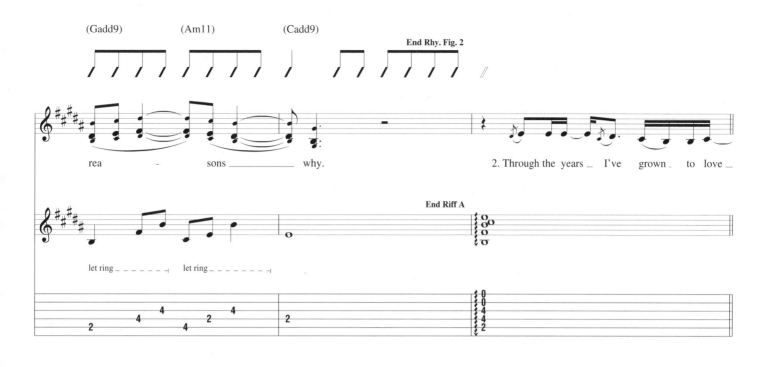

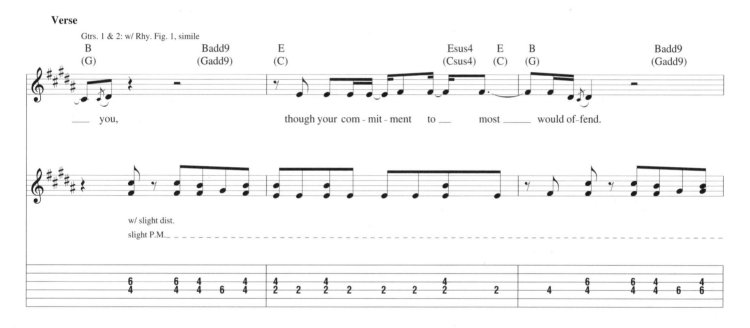

Verse

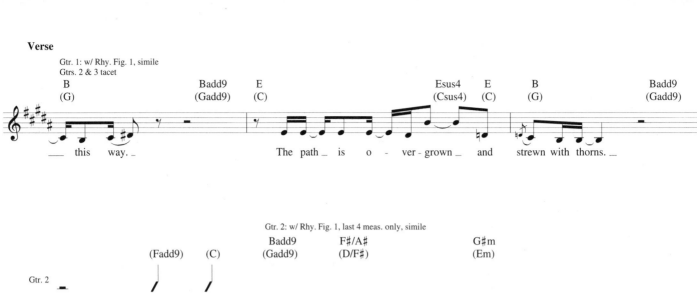

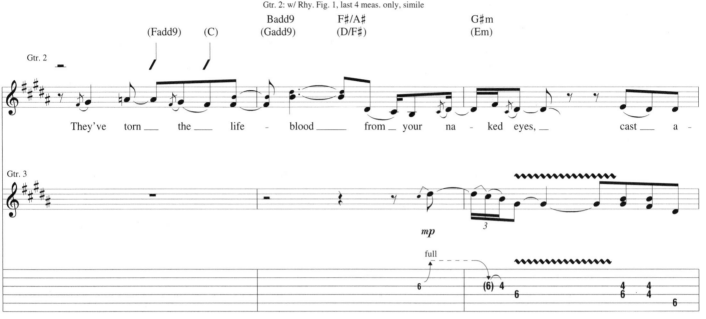

D.S. al Coda

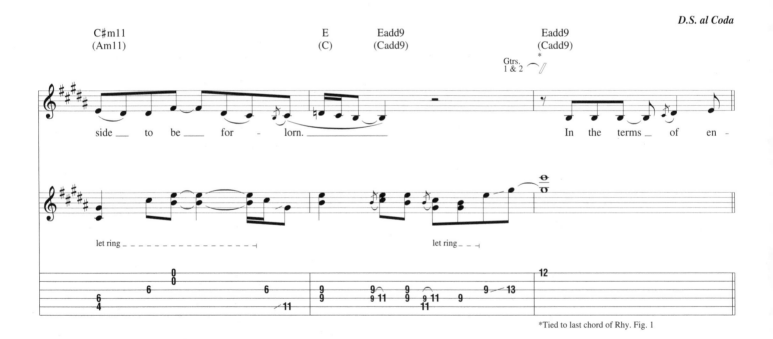

*Tied to last chord of Rhy. Fig. 1

Coda

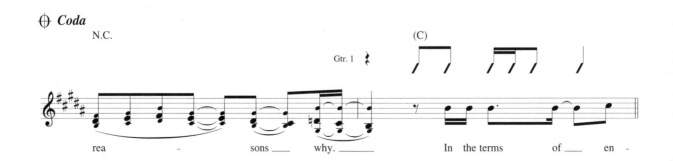

Chorus

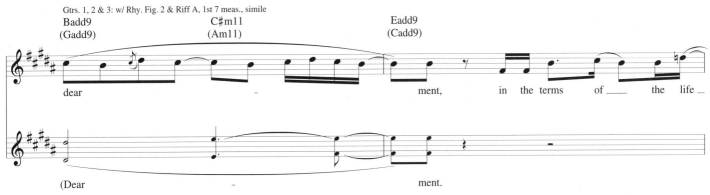

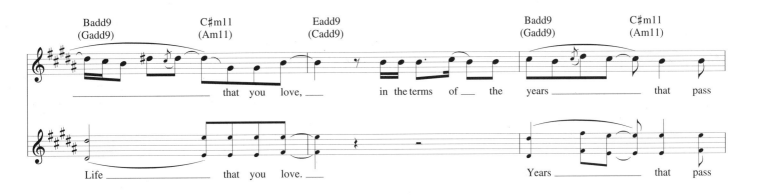

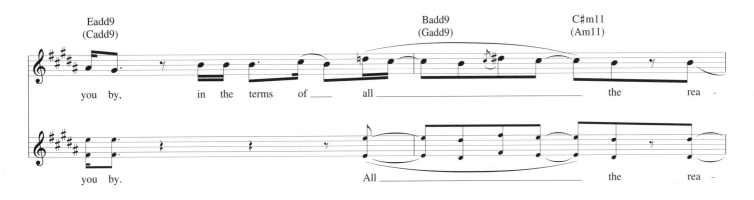

Bridge

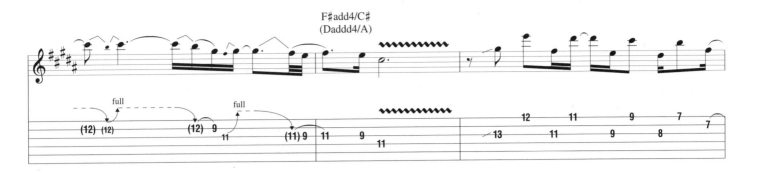

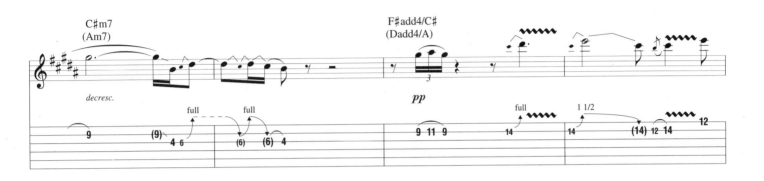

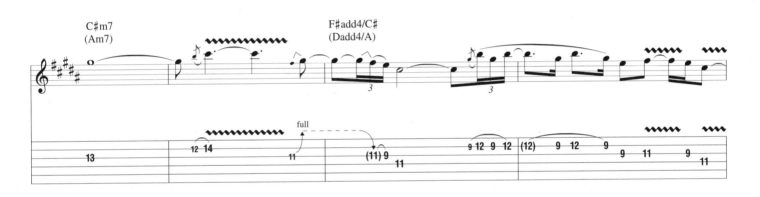

Fear

Words and Music by Sarah McLachlan

* Piano arr. for gtr.   ** Chord symbols reflect basic tonality.

* Ties into first beat of Rhy. Fig. 1

speaks to me of com - fort. But I

Chorus

fear I have noth - ing __ to give __ and I have so __ much to lose__

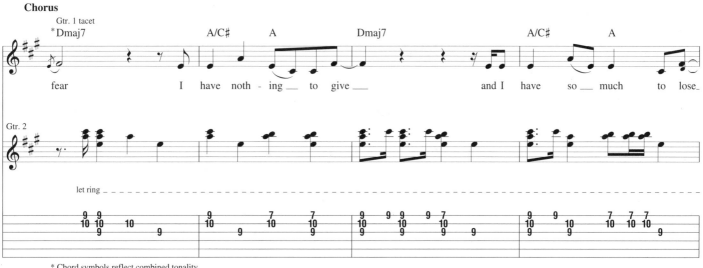

* Chord symbols reflect combined tonality.

__ here in __ this lone - ly place, __ tan - gled up __ in __ our __

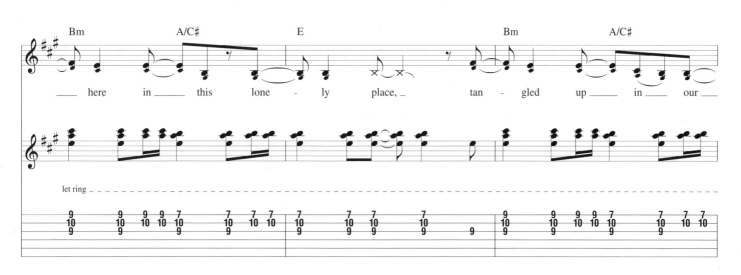

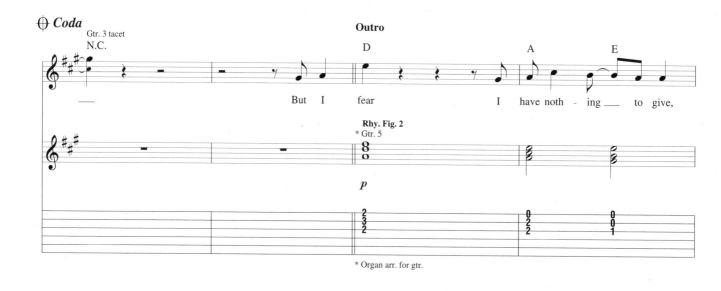

* Organ arr. for gtr.

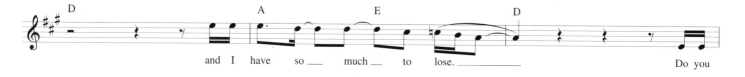

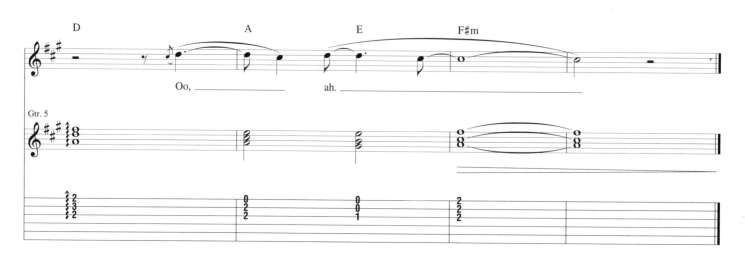

Possession

Words and Music by Sarah McLachlan

* Chord symbols reflect basic tonality.

** Two gtrs. arr. for one.

66

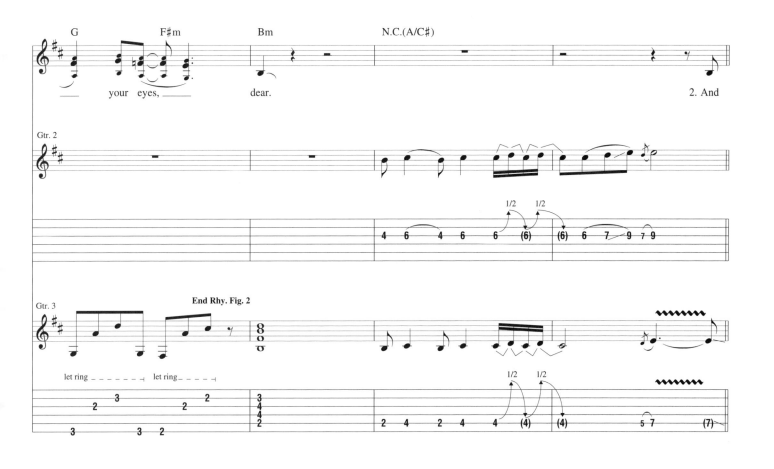

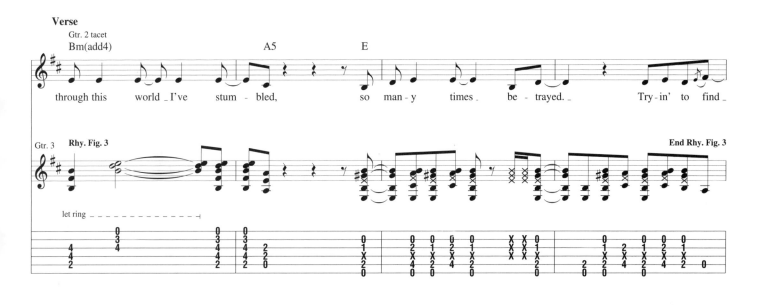

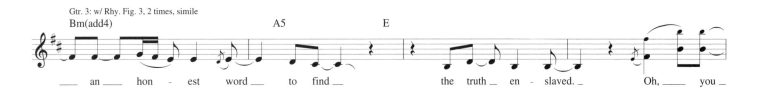

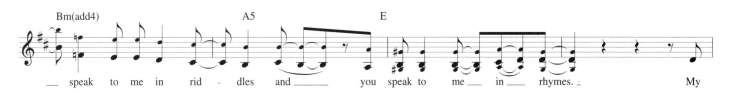

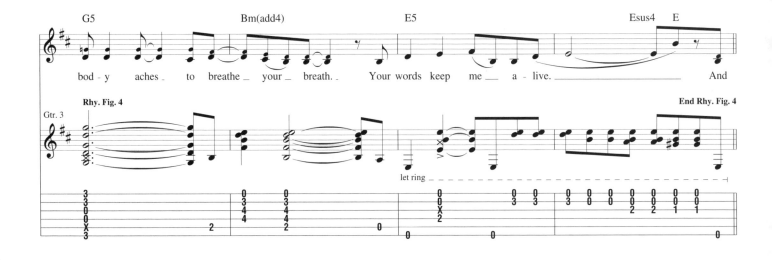

bod - y aches _ to breathe _ your _ breath. _ Your words keep me _ a - live. _ And

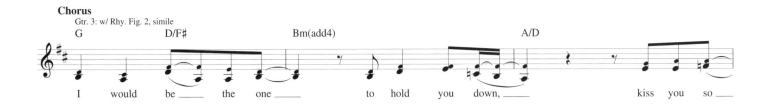

Chorus

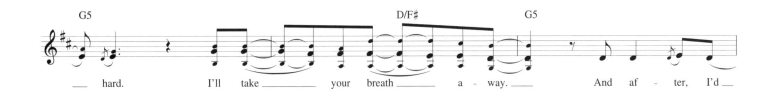

I would be _ the one _ to hold you down, _ kiss you so _

_ hard. I'll take _ your breath _ a - way. _ And af - ter, I'd

wipe a - way the tears. Just close _ your eyes. _

Guitar Solo

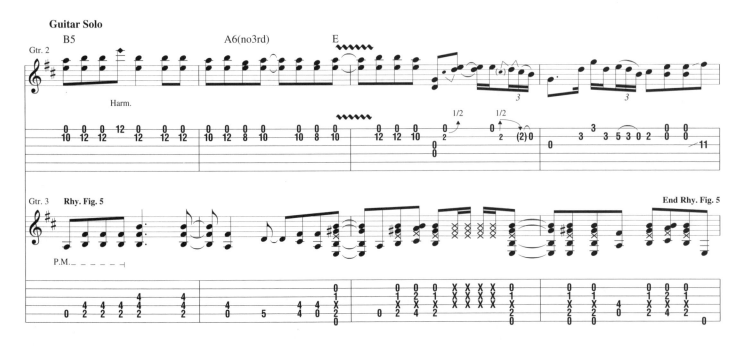

* Played behind the beat.

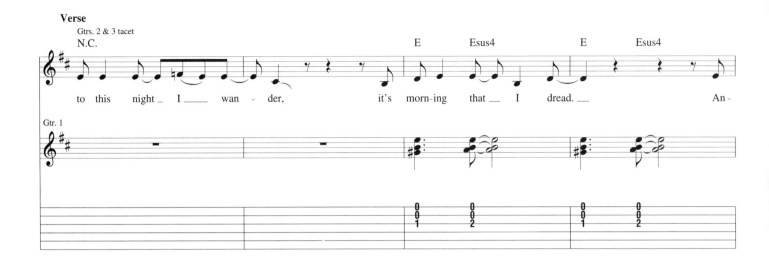

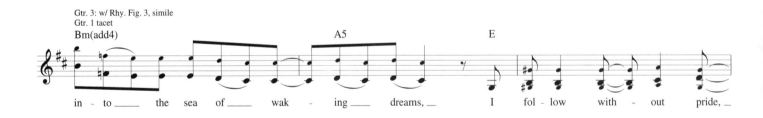

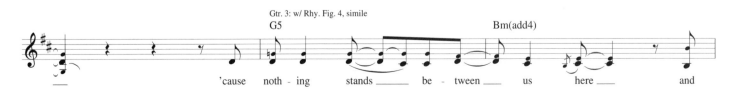

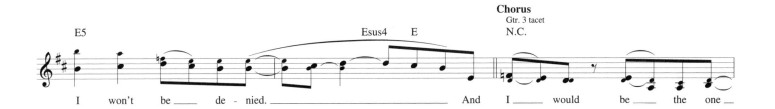

I won't be de-nied. And I would be the one

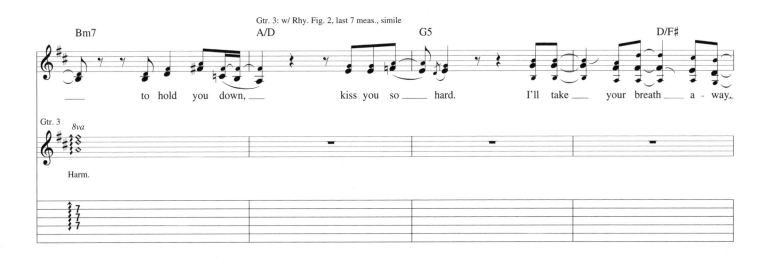

to hold you down, kiss you so hard. I'll take your breath a-way.

And af-ter, I'd wipe a-way the tears. Just close your eyes, dear,

and I'll hold you down, kiss you so hard. I'll

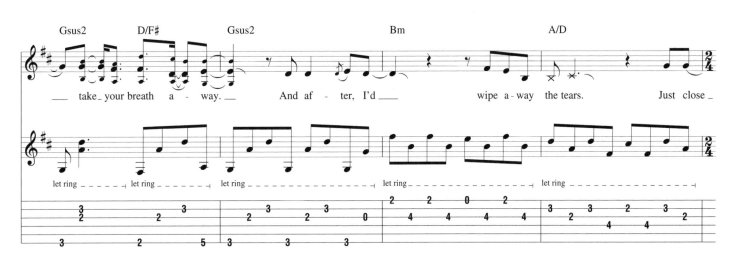

take your breath a-way. And af-ter, I'd wipe a-way the tears. Just close

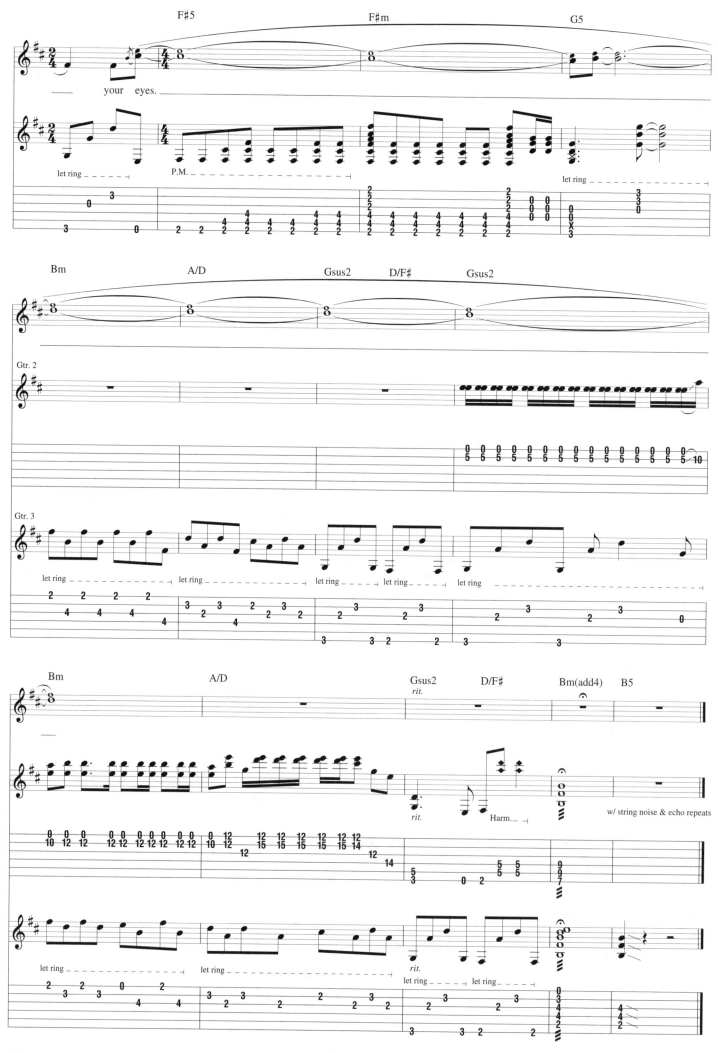

Sweet Surrender

Words and Music by Sarah McLachlan

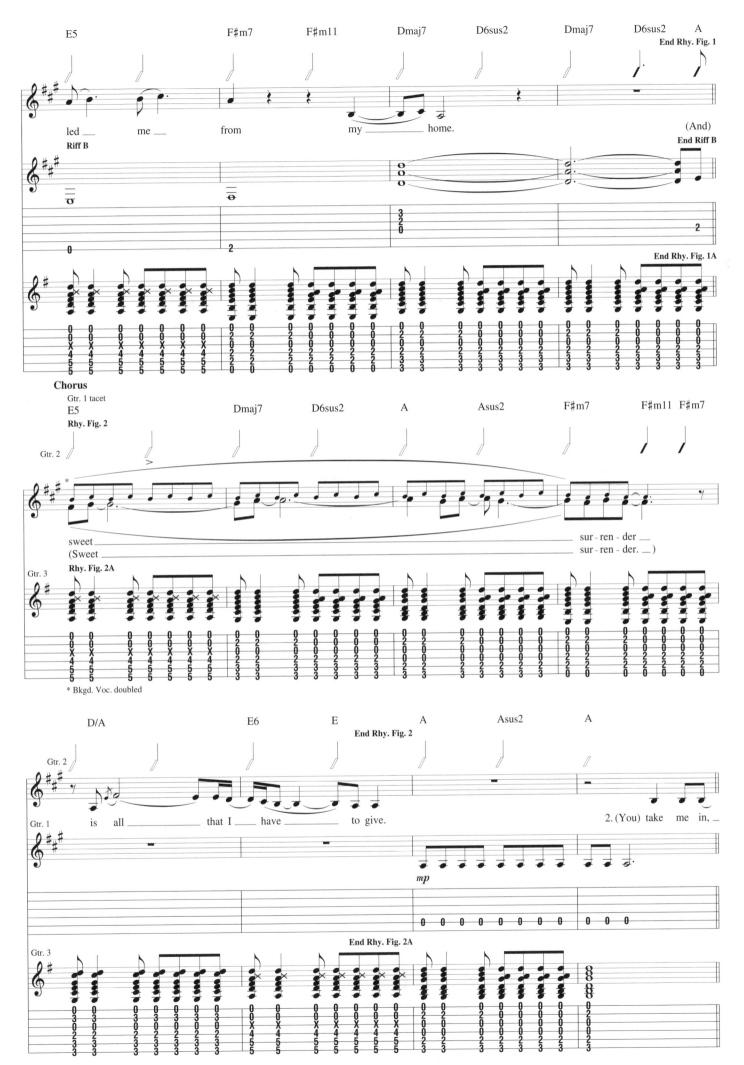

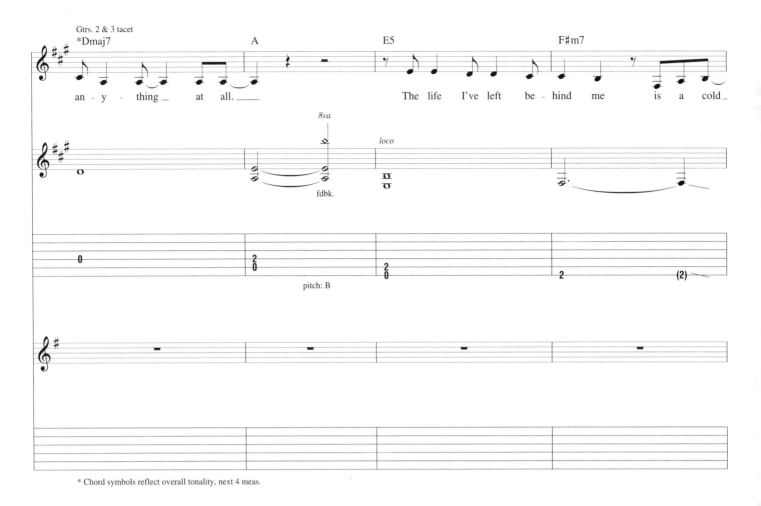

an-y-thing _ at all. ___ The life I've left be-hind me is a cold _

*Dmaj7   A   E5   F#m7

Gtrs. 2 & 3 tacet

8va

loco

fdbk.

pitch: B

* Chord symbols reflect overall tonality, next 4 meas.

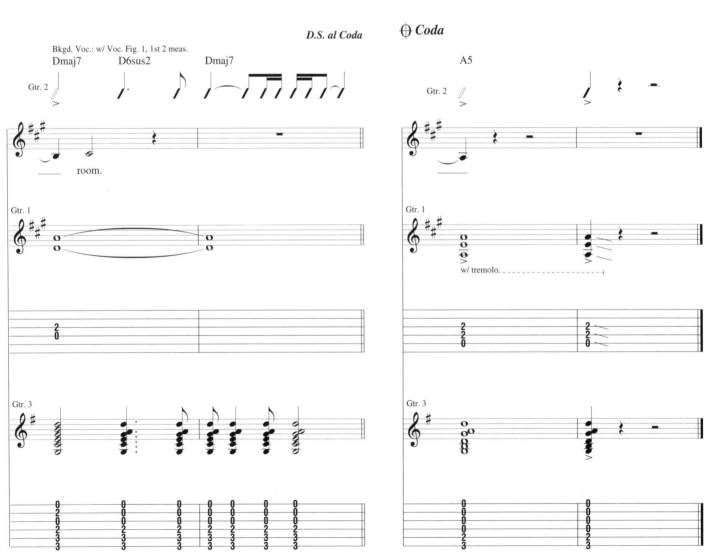

D.S. al Coda   **⊕ Coda**

Bkgd. Voc.: w/ Voc. Fig. 1, 1st 2 meas.

Dmaj7   D6sus2   Dmaj7   A5

Gtr. 2   Gtr. 2

room.

Gtr. 1   Gtr. 1

w/ tremolo

Gtr. 3   Gtr. 3

Ice Cream

Words and Music by Sarah McLachlan

Fumbling Towards Ecstasy

Words and Music by Sarah McLachlan and Pierre Marchand

Chorus

And if I shed a tear I won't cage it, __ I won't fear __ love.

No, and if I feel a rage, I won't de - ny it. __ I won't fear __ love.

Interlude

Fill 1

* w/ tremolo effect

* Chord is struck once while effect produces rhythm shown.

Verse

Gtr. 1: w/ Rhy. Fig. 1, 3 times

Em   Bm   A   Bm

2. Com-pan-ion to our de-mons, they will dance and we will play. With

Gtr. 2

Em   Bm   A   Bm

chairs, __ can-dles and clothes, mak-in' dark-ness __ in the day. It-'ll be

let ring

Em   Bm   A   Bm

eas-y _____ to look in or out, __ up-stream or down, __ with-out a thought. _____

let ring

(cont. in slash)

𝄋 Chorus

A5   D5   A5   Bm   Bsus2

Gtr. 2

simile on repeat

And if I shed a tear I won't cage it, __ I won't fear __ love.

Gtr. 1

mf

simile on repeat

let ring

No, and if I feel a rage, I won't de - ny it. __ I won't fear __ love.

Guitar Solo

Gtr. 1: w/ Rhy. Fig. 1, 1 3/4 times
Gtr. 2 tacet

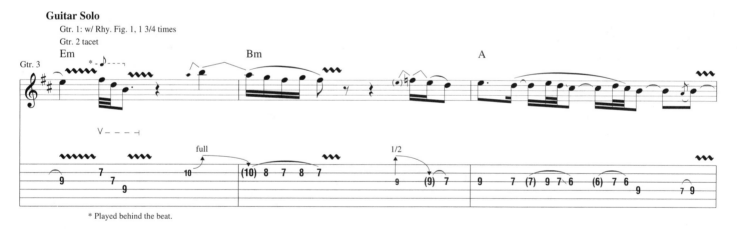

* Played behind the beat.

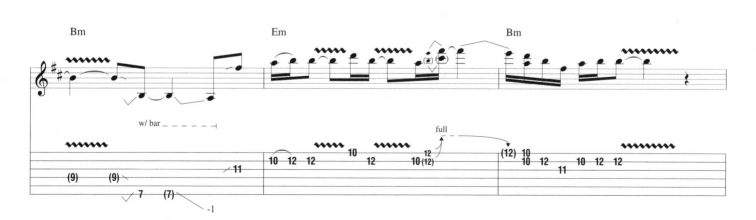

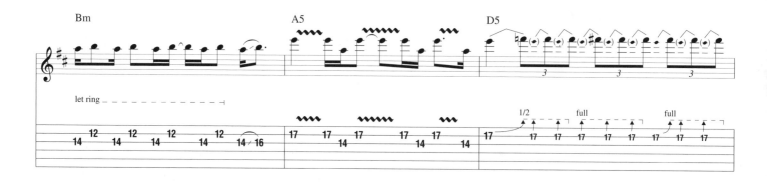

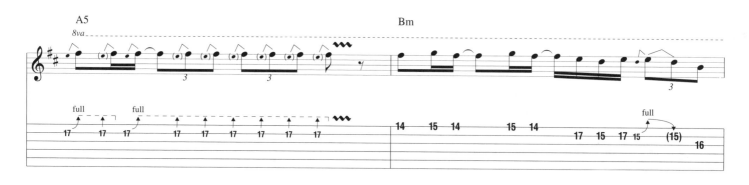

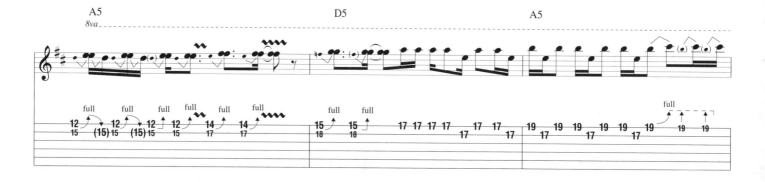

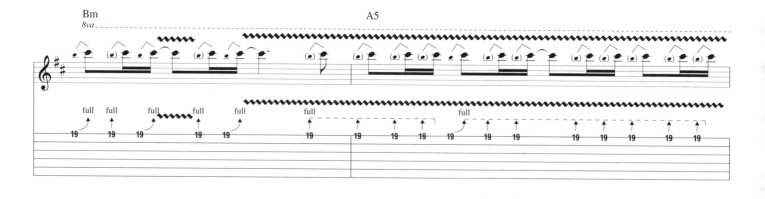

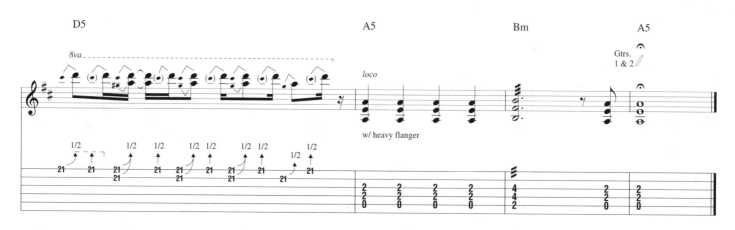

Angel

Words and Music by Sarah McLachlan

94